Peabody Public Library
Columbia City, IN

J 523.7 BELL
Bell, Trudy E.
The sun : our nearest star /
Trudy E. Bell.

NOV 5 '08

SO-ASH-480

DISCARD

The Sun: Our Nearest Star

Peabody Public Library
Columbia City, IN

TRUDY E. BELL

To the middle-schoolers of Messiah Lutheran School, especially my beloved Roxana

—T. E. B.

Published by Smart Apple Media, 1980 Lookout Drive, North Mankato, Minnesota 56003

Copyright © 2003 Byron Preiss Visual Publications
Printed in the United States of America
International copyright reserved in all countries. No part of this book may be reproduced in any form without written permission from the publisher.

Photo credits: Page 4: copyright © 1990-2003, Angelo-Australian Observatory, Photograph by David Malin. Page 6: courtesy NASA/Robert Gendler. Page 7: courtesy Royal Swedish Academy of Sciences. Page 8: courtesy MDI/SOHO Consortium/ESA/NASA. Page 9: NSO/AURA/NSF. Page 10: courtesy Royal Swedish Academy of Sciences. Page 11 (left): courtesy SOHO/MDI/Stanford U./ESA/NASA. Page 11 (right): courtesy T Rimmele/NSO/AURA/NSF. Page 12: courtesy GONG/NOAO. Page 14: courtesy NASA/SOHO. Page 15: courtesy MDI-SOI/SOHO Consortium/ESA/NASA. Page 17: from O. M. Mitchel's *Sidereal Messenger,* vol. 1, no. 3, September 1846. Page 18: from the article "The Eclipse Expedition in India," *The Illustrated London News*, January 20, 1872, p. 61 Page 20: from *Stars & Telescopes* by David P. Todd (Boston: Little, Brown & Co., 1899) Page 22: courtesy NSO/AUR/NSF. Page 23: courtesy NASA/GSFC. Page 24: courtesy SOHO/Extreme Ultraviolet Imaging Telescope (EIT) Consortium. Page 25: NSO/AURA/NSF. Page 26: courtesy SOHO/ Extreme Ultraviolet Imaging Telescope (EIT) Consortium. Page 28: courtesy LASCO/SOHO/ESA/NASA. Page 29: courtesy SOHO/NASA. Page 30: courtesy Steele Hill/SOHO/NASA. Page 32: courtesy NASA/Trygve Lindersen. Page 33: courtesy NSO/AURA/NSF. Page 34: copyright © 2003 George Jacoby, WIYN/NSF. Page 36: courtesy N.A.Sharp, NOAO/NSO/Kitt Peak FTS/AURA/NSF. Page 37: courtesy NASA/H. Bond. Page 38, 39: copyright © 2003 Trudy E. Bell. Page 41: copyright © 2003 Bill Livingston/NSO/AURA/NSF. Page 42: courtesy *Apollo 12* Crew/NASA
Cover art courtesy SOHO/EIT Consortium/ESA/NASA

Library of Congress Cataloging-in-Publication Data
Bell, Trudy E.
The sun: our nearest star / by Trudy E. Bell.
p. cm. — (The new solar system)
Summary: What if the sun went dark?—The sun's blemished face—The sun's "engine room"—The expedition that "discovered" the sun—The sun's ghostly atmosphere—The sun-earth connection—The sun as a "middle-aged" star—"Chasing" solar eclipses and other projects. Includes bibliographical references.

ISBN 1-58340-286-1
1. Sun—Juvenile literature. [1. Sun.] I. Title. II. Series.
QB521.5.B44 2003   523.7—dc21   2003042413

First Edition

9 8 7 6 5 4 3 2 1

Contents

The Sun appears to move from east to west because
Earth rotates. The Sun's brilliance, however, makes
it difficult to capture a "sun-trail"—the path the Sun
traces across the sky. To make this photograph, a
very dark filter covered a camera lens for several
hours while the shutter was left open; just after
sunset but before the sky was dark, the thick filter
was removed, allowing the camera to capture the
silhouetted landscape. The small flares along the
trail are where the Sun went behind thin clouds.

What if the Sun Went Dark?

What if, one fine summer day, by some impossible magic, the Sun simply stopped shining—as suddenly as if someone had switched off an electric light?

Instantly, every place on Earth would be blanketed by night. Without reflected sunlight, the Moon would be invisible except as a black disk silhouetted against a background of stars. Within days, crops the world over would be frosted and die. Within weeks, creeks and ponds would freeze solid, followed soon by lakes and large rivers. Within months, the Gulf Stream current in the Atlantic Ocean that warms the eastern United States and western Europe would stop flowing, and ice floes would spread in the Atlantic and the Pacific from the poles toward the tropics. After a year of eternal night, the oceans at temperate latitudes would be frozen as solidly as they are in the Arctic and the Antarctic, and glaciers would grow over all the continents. As Earth radiated away its remaining heat into the blackness of space, oxygen itself would freeze out of the air, falling gently like snow, and the air's nitrogen would liquefy and puddle on the frigid ground.

But by then, no one would be around to notice that the air was getting thin and unbreathable— virtually all plant and animal life on Earth would have long since frozen or starved to death. Indeed, if the Sun were blotted out for just one short month, no human would be left alive to tell the tale.

The Sun is the source of life on Earth. Many ancient cultures recognized that and worshiped the Sun as a god. Its heat warms our planet enough to keep water liquid, whether in life-giving rains or in seafood-rich oceans. Its light allows photosynthesis, so green plants can bear delicious fruits and exhale the oxygen that sustains life for animals. Its energy powers winds, ocean currents, and weather.

But what makes the Sun shine? How long will the Sun live? And what do daily, monthly, and yearly changes in the Sun mean for Earth?

Peabody Public Library
Columbia City, IN

5

The Sun is an extremely large ball of hot gas whose surface is
ceaselessly bubbling and seething. Most of the gas is hydrogen
(this photograph was taken in the red light emitted by
hydrogen at the wavelength called hydrogen-alpha).
The surface is mottled with convection cells
called granules. Brighter regions with
dark spots are sunspots.

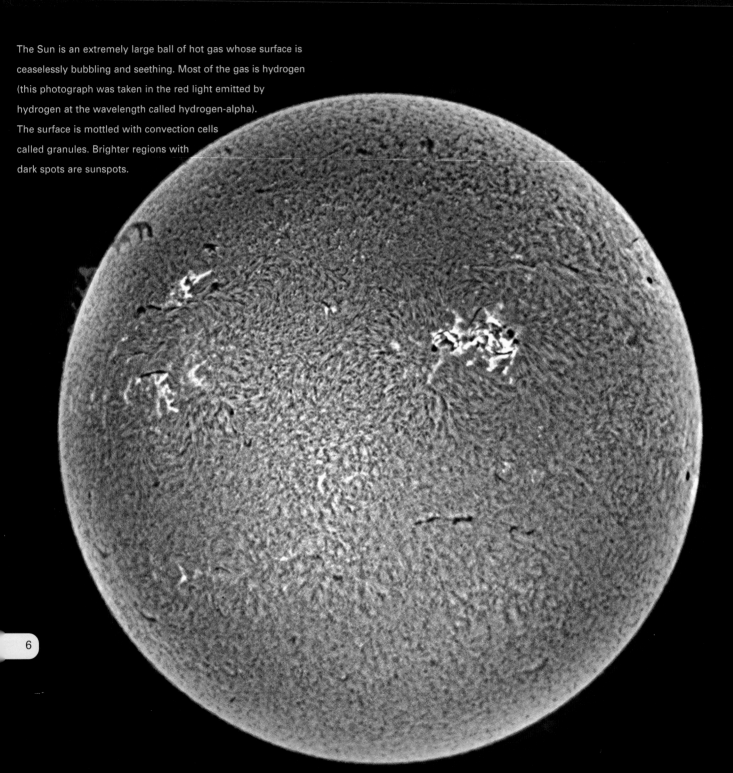

CHAPTER ONE

The Sun's Blemished Face

Outside on a sunny day, curl your forefinger against your thumb to make a pinhole-sized hole. Point that hole toward the Sun and let it cast an image of the Sun onto the palm of your other hand. Because you should not look directly at the Sun, the pinhole acts as a lens. With your hands, you've just made a crude pinhole camera.

What do you see? Chances are, you'll see simply a pale yellowish disk. That's the photosphere, the Sun's visible surface (from the Greek word *photo*, meaning "light"). Actually, that glowing surface is a layer only some 250 miles (400 km) thick, extraordinarily thin compared with the 420,000-mile (700,000 km) radius of the entire Sun—far thinner in proportion to the Sun than the thickness of the skin on a large apple.

Look closely at the image on your palm. Do you see any tiny dark spots? If so, you may be seeing sunspots: colossal magnetic storms raging in the photosphere—hurricanes of electrified gas so enormous that they could swallow Earth several times over (some are more than 30,000 miles [50,000 km] in diameter).

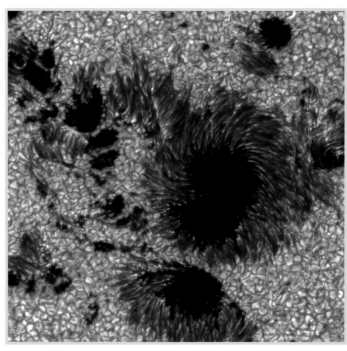

This group of sunspots, observed on July 15, 2002, shows details in their structure as small as 60 miles (90 km) in diameter. The central part of each sunspot (the umbra) looks dark because the strong magnetic fields there stop upwelling hot gas from the solar interior, so the region is cooler than most of the Sun's surface. The lighter, thread-like structures surrounding the umbra make up the penumbra.

7

Every now and then, an area near a large sunspot will explode, releasing many times more energy than an atomic bomb. That's a solar flare, blasting super-hot material far into space in just a few minutes. Some of that energy also heads downward, into the Sun's surface, creating "sun quakes"— shock waves that spread out across the photosphere like ripples in a pond created by a tossed stone.

Sunspots look darker than the surrounding photosphere because they are somewhat cooler. But don't be deceived. Sunspots are plenty hot—about 6,500°F (3,400°C)— and glowing. But because the rest of the Sun's surface is a blistering 10,000°F (5,500°C), the cooler sunspots appear dark, in the same way a glowing candle flame on Earth casts a shadow in bright sunlight.

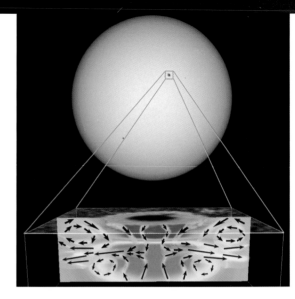

What's under a sunspot? The space-based Solar and Heliospheric Observatory (SOHO) reveals that immediately below a sunspot material flows inward (dark arrows). The converging undertow pulls surface material toward the spot and prevents the concentrated magnetic fields from flying apart (as repelling poles of iron magnets would), keeping the sunspot together.

The fact that the Sun's face occasionally breaks out into sunspots has been known since 1612, when Galileo Galilei and several of his contemporaries first turned crude telescopes toward the Sun. For a couple of years, Galileo (who did not look directly at the blinding Sun but safely projected dimmer images of the Sun onto a screen) systematically made drawings of the spots day after day. He found that while small spots might grow and die in a few days, large spots can persist for a month or more.

He also found that the spots don't stay in one place on the Sun. Each day they move a little farther from one edge toward the other, eventually disappearing around the Sun's western limb, foreshortening (appearing to be compressed by the viewing perspective from Earth) as they approach the western limb. From this, Galileo inferred that the Sun is a sphere.

Not only that, the Sun is a rotating sphere—because about two weeks after particularly large and

Solar flares, such as this one that erupted in February 1998, are violent storms on the Sun's surface that can eject particles and emit radiation toward Earth, affecting radio communication. Flares are generally correlated with the eleven-year solar activity or sunspot cycle, becoming more common as the Sun approaches solar maximum.

recognizable sunspots disappeared around the western limb, they would reappear again at the eastern limb for another journey across the Sun's face. In fact, Galileo found, the Sun rotates about once every 27 days.

But the Sun, which is a huge ball of hot gases, does not have a solid surface. The sunspots themselves revealed that. On a rigid planet such as Earth, all latitudes, from the equator to the poles, rotate together—just like all the features on a basketball spinning on your fingertip. On the Sun, however, the equator is running a race that it always wins: Sunspots at the solar equator complete one rotation in less than 25 days, while those at higher latitudes (closer to the poles) may take closer to 30 days. What causes this weird differential rotation is still something of a mystery. (It's also characteristic of gas giant planets such as Jupiter.)

Dark sunspots are only the most obvious features on the Sun's face. The photosphere is also dotted with bright *faculae* (Latin for "little torches"), magnetic areas that are like sunspots concentrated in much smaller areas and that often form over areas where sunspots will later appear. While sunspots look dark, faculae look bright and are most easily spotted against the relatively dark limb of the Sun.

Solar telescopes on Earth and in space have revealed the Sun's visible surface to be a restless ocean of

New Sunspot Structures Discovered

In 2002, new solar structures were discovered with the aid of a new Swedish, 40-inch (1 meter) solar telescope on La Palma in the Canary Islands. Three of the panels below show small sunspots called "pores" that have thin dark lines around their edges called "hairs." The surrounding solar surface shows dark lines dubbed "canals." The fourth panel (d) shows filaments from the sunspot's penumbra with dark cores; also, one of the filaments seems to be twisted. The tick marks around the edge of the image show the scale; distance between two neighboring ticks is 600 miles (1,000 km).

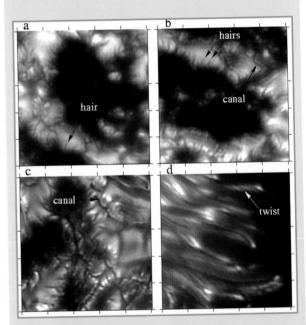

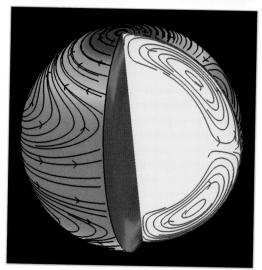

SOHO revealed that hot, electrically charged gas flows along and beneath the Sun's surface as solar rivers—the equatorial regions (red on this map) flow faster than the polar regions (blue). Hot gas moves from the equator to the poles, while internal eddies circulate gas from deep inside the Sun.

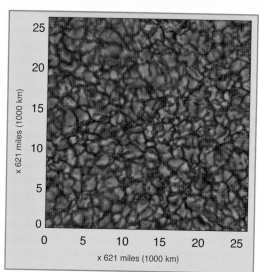

x 621 miles (1000 km)

x 621 miles (1000 km)

This is a close-up view of the network of solar granules—sometimes called "rice grains" because of their appearance. In each granule, hot material from the solar interior wells up to the surface, explodes, fragments, and decays in an average of 20 minutes.

gases, ceaselessly spitting, erupting, and vibrating. The entire photosphere (except where sunspots reside) is seething with granules—convection cells the size of the state of California or Texas—in which hot fluid rises from the Sun's interior, spreads out across the surface, cools, and then sinks inward again in a process called convection, all within about 20 minutes. The entire photosphere is also roiling with supergranules—huge convection cells rivaling sunspots in size. Meanwhile, patches of the Sun chaotically oscillate up and down in cycles of about five minutes. Simultaneously, sound waves generated inside the Sun by pressure fluctuations bounce off the inner surface of the photosphere, setting the Sun vibrating in millions of different patterns, virtually "ringing" like a bell.

In short, between churning sunspots, exploding flares, sun quakes, rising and sinking convection cells, and erratic acoustic vibrations, standing on the Sun's surface would be like trying to surf on flowing volcanic lava during an earthquake!

The Sun continually oscillates or vibrates like a ringing gong. Large patches of the Sun vibrate in and out, back and forth, even as the Sun rotates. One mode of solar oscillation is shown here, with blue indicating patches moving outward and red indicating patches moving inward. Just as earthquakes reveal much about Earth's interior, solar surface vibrations reveal much about our home star's density, temperature, motion, and chemical composition.

The Sun's "Engine Room"

If the Sun's visible surface is only 250 miles (400 km) thick, what's hidden beneath it? What do sunspots, convection cells, acoustic vibrations, and analysis of solar radiation at all wavelengths reveal about the Sun's innards?

Let's take a virtual trip from the center of the Sun.

We begin in the Sun's core, the "engine room," where thermonuclear reactions consume hydrogen to form helium. It's sweltering hot in this fiery nuclear furnace—a good 27 *million*°F (15 million°C). We're also under crushing pressure: The Sun's core is 10 times denser than lead. If a person were to heft a teaspoonful of this solar material on Earth, it would weigh several pounds!

Watch out for flying protons! Although the atomic form of hydrogen—the lightest and most abundant element in the universe—normally consists of one proton and one electron, in the Sun's core, the heat, density, and pressure have long since ionized (stripped away) each atom's electron. So the bare nuclei (positively charged protons) are slamming around, colliding into one another with so much energy that they overcome their repulsive electrical force and fuse (stick) together, forming nuclei of a completely different element: helium. This nuclear fusion (union of lightweight atomic nuclei at high pressure to form heavier nuclei) releases blinding energy, duplicated on Earth in the devastating hydrogen bomb. The Sun is "burning" several hundred million tons of hydrogen every *second*—but it has so much hydrogen that it won't run out for another 5 billion years.

Let's begin drifting up toward the Sun's surface and watch how conditions change. As we rise, the temperature drops and the pressure becomes less crushing. In fact, 25 percent of the way up from the center of the Sun (about 105,000 miles, or 175,000 km), the temperature is about half of what it is in the core (12.5 million°F, or 7 million°C) and the density is about an eighth of what it is in the core. Here nuclear fusion is almost completely shut off, meaning we're now at the outer edge of the Sun's core.

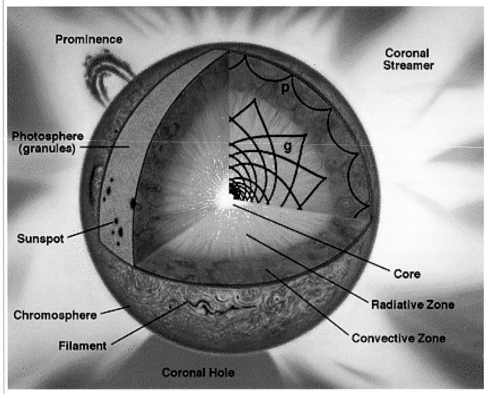

Prominence

Coronal Streamer

p

g

Photosphere (granules)

Sunspot

Chromosphere

Filament

Coronal Hole

Core

Radiative Zone

Convective Zone

This cutaway diagram of the Sun shows the structure of its interior. The core is its nuclear furnace, where hydrogen fusing into helium releases energy. The energy travels outward through the radiative and convective zones to the photosphere, and then out into space through the Sun's chromosphere and corona. Astronomers infer the structure and composition of the Sun's interior by watching how sound waves (lettered p and g) disturb its surface.

Continuing upward, we're entering a fairly tranquil region called the radiative zone, which extends from the outer edge of the core to about 70 percent of the way up from the center of the Sun (about 294,000 miles, or 470,000 km, from the center). Here the energy generated in the core is radiated, or simply glows, emitting photons (particles of light) that travel at the speed of light—meaning they could directly cross the 189,000-mile (300,000 km) layer in little more than a second. However, the solar material is still so dense that the photons keep bouncing from particle to particle, getting absorbed, reradiated, and rerouted. Indeed, it can take up to *a million years* for an individual photon to make it through the radiative zone.

Leaving this area, we enter the thin interface layer, or tachocline, which separates the Sun's relatively tranquil radiative zone from the swirling, circulating convective zone. Moreover, the tachocline appears to be the source of the Sun's magnetic field—and magnetism plays a vital role in the Sun's design, as well as in the Sun's interaction with Earth.

At last we come to the convective zone: At the bottom of this zone, the Sun's temperature is a mere 3.6 million°F (2 million°C). This temperature is cool enough for heavier trace elements (such as carbon, nitrogen, oxygen, calcium, and iron) to hold on to some of their electrons. But that makes this layer more opaque, so it's harder for photons to radiate through it, as they do in the radiative zone. That, in turn, traps heat, making the dense gaseous fluid unstable—so it starts to convect, or boil. Masses of material rise toward the Sun's surface quite rapidly, expanding and cooling.

Moving closer to the surface, we reach the photosphere. Note that here the gas's temperature has dropped to 10,000°F (5,500°C)—the Sun's surface temperature measured from Earth—and its density is less than that of the air atop Mount Everest.

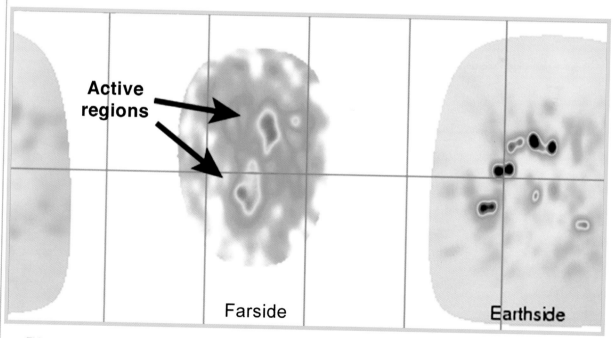

Active regions

Farside

Earthside

This map of the Sun was made by the SOHO spacecraft on April 12, 2001. On the left is a map of the hemisphere opposite Earth, tracking the largest group of sunspots seen in a decade (large, yellow-ringed red area). On the right is a map of the calculated strengths of magnetic fields on the hemisphere of the Sun facing Earth.

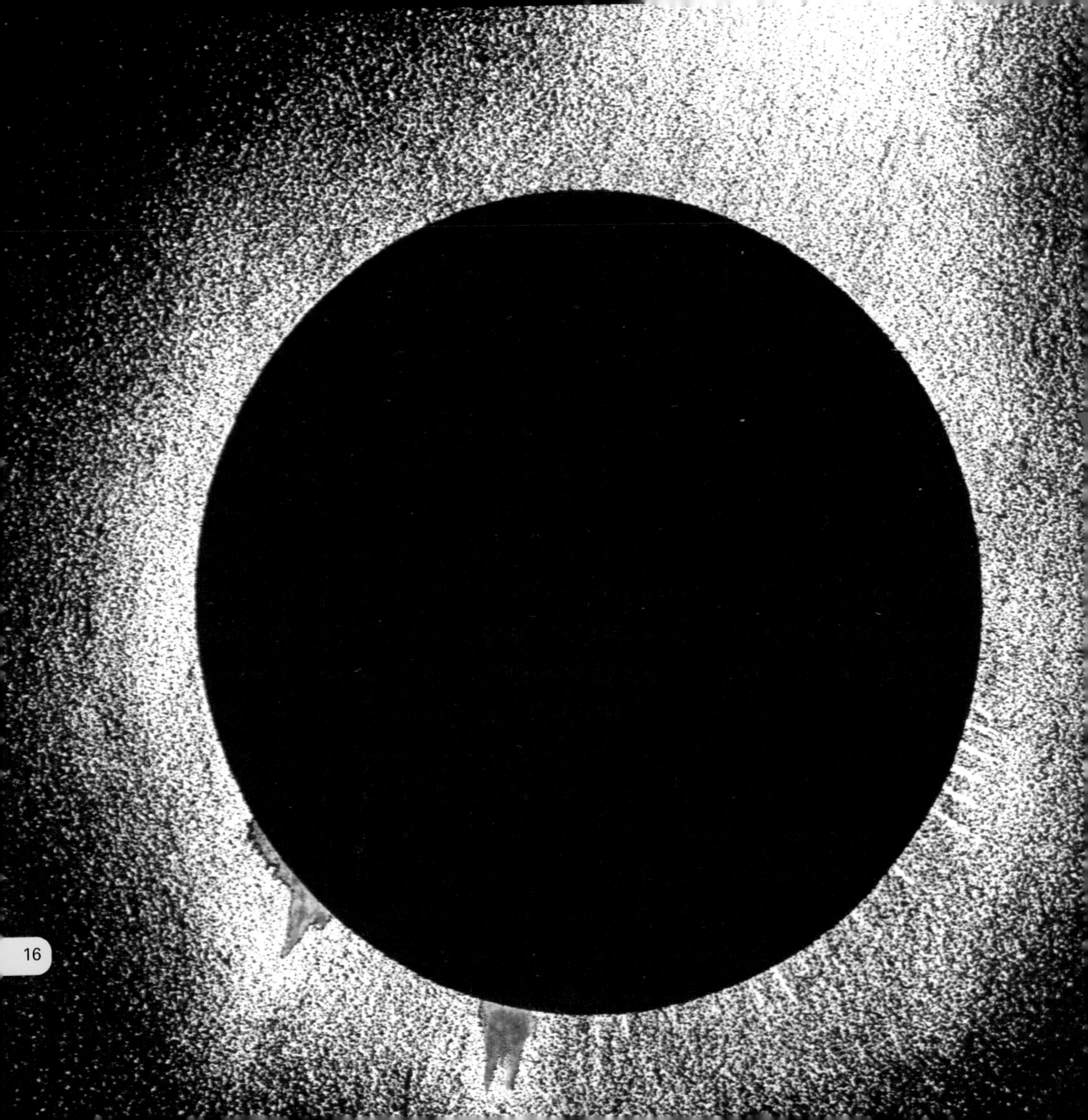

The Expedition That "Discovered" the Sun

Our virtual journey from the Sun's core to the photosphere explores only half of the Sun. To investigate the Sun's outer atmosphere, above the photosphere, let's take a different type of virtual journey—back more than a century-and-a-half ago.

Thursday, July 8, 1842, dawned as a fine summer morning across southern Europe. From hotels and camp tents scattered across hundreds of miles of southern France and northern Italy, astronomers rolled off beds and cots and looked up at the cloudless sky with anticipation, padding outdoors to adjust their telescopes and check their clocks. They all eagerly awaited the day's momentous event: a total eclipse of the Sun.

The astronomers knew that roughly a couple of times a year, the Moon—the closest major body to Earth—passes in front of the Sun, partially blocking its light. Such partial eclipses usually occur almost unnoticed. But on this day in southern Europe, the Moon would *completely* block the Sun's light, plunging Earth into night for a few minutes at midday.

The astronomers were excited. The Moon and the Sun were essential for finding latitudes and longitudes on land and at sea. A total solar eclipse offered an unusual chance to check the Moon's actual position in the sky against mathematical predictions and to accurately position into one map the locations of various European cities within the

During the total solar eclipse of July 8, 1842, this stunning sight of the eclipsed Sun (as drawn by Austrian astronomer Wilhelm von Biela before the days of photography) astounded astronomers all across Europe. For the first time, they saw brilliant "red protuberances" (prominences) frozen in suspended leaps around the black disk of the moon, which was completely surrounded by the ghostly white corona.

eclipse's path of totality. For months, the astronomers had been training and preparing themselves to time the instants the leading and trailing edges of the new Moon would cover and uncover the Sun's brilliant face.

Townspeople across France and Italy were also excited. Never before had so many strangers with so many odd-looking pieces of equipment descended on their sleepy farm villages. Everyone turned out to watch the clusters of scholars, as well as to squint up at the Sun, toward which all the instruments were pointing.

First contact! Through filtered telescopes, astronomers could see the leading edge of the Moon make the first nick in the edge of the Sun— a nick that slowly grew as if it were a cookie being bitten. In about an hour, the landscape was noticeably dimmed as the Moon had obscured 95 percent of the Sun's light . . . 98 percent . . . 99 percent . . . totality!

As complete darkness fell, a cry rose up from the townspeople, who fell to their knees, praying in French, Italian, and Latin, lifting their clasped hands heavenward.

Startled, the astronomers glanced up—and their own jaws dropped. As they had expected, the black disk of the Moon hung in the star-spangled midday sky. To their astonishment, however, its circumference was

The average Victorian eclipse expedition was a very big deal, some involving dozens of telescopes and observers. Some even had very permanent-looking "temporary" observatories with photographic darkrooms complete with running water (this in an age when most homes did not have indoor plumbing).

On this peculiar 19th-century machine, invented by astronomer David Peck Todd of Amherst College Observatory, 20 telescopes tracked the Sun across the sky. Cameras mounted on each telescope took photographs of the eclipsed Sun; the timing of each exposure was controlled by a perforated sheet of paper similar to those used for music in player pianos. With his setup, Todd was able to snap more than 300 photos in less than 3 minutes.

dotted with brilliant ruby flames suspended in contorted loops. Even more astounding, all around the bizarre spectacle was a gossamer, pearly halo of arresting beauty.

A precious minute or two later, as the trailing edge of the Moon uncovered the edge of the Sun, the mysterious apparitions disappeared in the Sun's dazzling brilliance.

The astronomers were stunned—as stunned as the frightened, uneducated populace weeping and murmuring prayers in the dusty roads around them. They clamored with questions: What were those magnificent and wholly unexpected marvels? Were they real, or just some kind of optical illusion? If real, were they part of the Sun or the Moon? What caused them? And why were they visible only when the Sun was totally eclipsed?

They determined to take advantage of every future total solar eclipse to discover more about the physical nature of the Sun—no matter how short the totality, how great the distance from home, or how difficult the journey.

Arguably, July 8, 1842, was the date solar physics was born—the day astronomers began questing after the physical nature of the Sun rather than just tracking its position in the sky.

By 1900, special solar telescopes for photographing the eclipsed Sun had become so enormous they had to be laid horizontally on the ground! The all-time biggest heliostat, as they were called, had a lens 12 inches (30 cm) in diameter that brought light to a focus 135 feet (41 m) away (longest white tube right of the center of photo).

The Sun's delicately structured outer corona is visible to the unaided eye only during a total solar eclipse. Here is how it appeared during the solar eclipse of March 7, 1970. The path of totality swept across Mexico and up the east coast of the United States.

CHAPTER FOUR

The Sun's Ghostly Atmosphere

DISCARD

The 1842 total solar eclipse was the first to be viewed by a large number of trained observers. And it spurred hundreds of other expeditions throughout the rest of the 19th century to the present day. Thousands of astronomers traveled from Europe and the United States into North and South America, the Pacific Islands, and Asia, risking life and limb for fleeting glimpses of the mysterious "red protuberances" and ghostly white corona then seen only during a total eclipse. By the end of the 19th century, they learned that these were two previously unknown layers of the Sun above the photosphere—invisible except when the photosphere's blinding brilliance was blocked by the Moon.

The thin, irregular layer immediately above the photosphere is the chomosphere. It contains the red flame-like prominences, which are cooler and denser jets of electrified gas erupting and suspended by loops in the Sun's magnetic field. In the chromosphere, the Sun's temperature—after having cooled all the way from the core to the photosphere—begins rising again, from 10,000°F (5,500°C) to 36,000°F (20,000°C). At those hotter

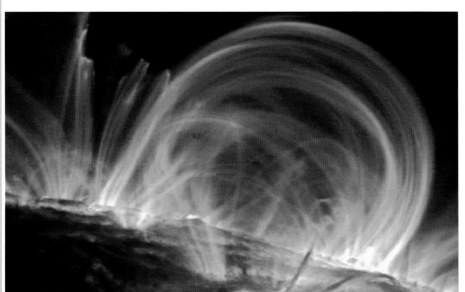

Coronal loops—fountains of multimillion-degree, electrified gas—spurt from low in the Sun's corona. There, 10,000 miles (16,000 km) above the photosphere, gas is heated to temperatures 300 times higher than that of the Sun's visible surface. Some coronal loops arch more than 300,000 miles (500,000 km) high along magnetic fields.

23

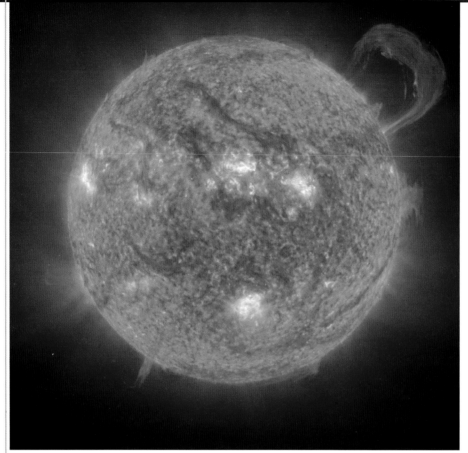

A huge handle-shaped, gaseous prominence (upper right) erupted from the Sun hundreds of thousands of miles into space on September 14, 1999 and was photographed by SOHO. Every feature in this image traces a magnetic field structure; hottest areas appear almost white, whereas cooler areas are darker red.

temperatures, hydrogen glows with pure, reddish light called H-alpha emission. The striking ruby color, in fact, is what gives the chromosphere its name (*chromo-* is a Greek prefix for "color").

Many prominences are so enormous that they could swallow our entire planet. Some can even extend farther than half the diameter of the Sun. When seen projected as darker, threadlike structures against the body of the Sun, prominences are called filaments. Prominences and filaments are part of the weblike chromospheric network that outlines supergranule cells in the photosphere below. Fluid convection within a supergranule clusters the Sun's magnetic field lines toward its edges, outlining its size and shape. These everchanging bundles of field lines outlining the supergranule boundaries reach up through the chromosphere, producing the chromospheric network.

The chromospheric network also includes *plages* (French for "beach"), which are bright patches surrounding sunspots, and spicules, which are small, spiky, jetlike eruptions that last a few minutes.

Above the chromosphere is the mysterious transition region—another thin, irregular layer of the Sun's atmosphere. Most of the Sun's light is emitted not by hydrogen but by heavier elements—notably carbon, oxygen, silicon, and sulfur. Due to the intense heat and pressure, each of these elements is so highly ionized that it is missing three or more electrons. At 180,000 to 360,000°F (100,000 to 200,000°C), the Sun's light glows as ultraviolet wavelengths that can be seen only from above Earth's atmosphere in space.

Lastly, above the transition region is the even hotter solar corona, the Sun's gorgeous outer atmosphere. Its name, Latin for "crown," is apt, as during total solar eclipses it surrounds the black disk of the Moon as a beautiful, pearly halo. Its shape changes from one eclipse to another, having just a few quiet streamers extending from the Sun's equator at solar minimum (years of few or no sunspots) but spiking out from around the entire disk of the Sun at solar maximum (years of many sunspots).

Although the corona can extend a dozen solar diameters—some 5 million miles (8 million km)—from the Sun, at 1.8 million°F (1 million°C), it's as hot as the Sun's interior. And as inside the Sun, at those

Gas in the Sun's chromosphere (thin, red layer just above the photosphere) is so hot that it is ionized: that is, its molecules are stripped of electrons and thus have an electric charge. Such a hot, ionized gas is called a plasma. The distinctive curved shape of many solar prominences results from strong magnetic fields in the region bending the solar plasma into a loop.

Active regions on the Sun are ones with clusters of strong magnetic fields. At wavelengths of light, sunspots might be visible. At extreme ultraviolet wavelengths, however, as shown here in this composite image of three wavelengths from SOHO in 1998, the active regions are very bright.

high temperatures, even the atoms of heavy elements such as iron have been ionized, or stripped of most electrons. Thus, the corona is mostly charged particles—negatively charged electrons and positively charged nuclei, not only of hydrogen and helium but also of carbon, nitrogen, oxygen, iron, and other elements (which have been created by fusion of helium and heavier nuclei).

But, completely defying common sense, if you were able to stick your hand into the Sun's million-degree corona, it would not even feel hot! That's because, unlike the Sun's superdense core, the corona is so rarefied that it's scarcely denser than the vacuum of interplanetary space. To a physicist, temperature is a measure of the energy (speed) of individual particles. But to your skin, perception of temperature also depends on the density of the particles. That's why hot water feels hotter to your skin than air at the same temperature, even though the air molecules have the same energy as the water molecules: Water is denser, so more molecules are bouncing off (and thus conveying their energy to) each square inch of your skin.

Coronal loops and streamers—such as prominences and filaments—concentrate at the equatorial, or middle, latitudes above sunspots and other active regions of the Sun, sometimes lasting days or even weeks. But for reasons still not well understood, x-ray images from solar observatories in space reveal that the corona also has "holes," mostly over the Sun's higher latitudes and polar regions.

How the Sun's outer layers—the chromosphere, the transition region, and the corona—could be so much hotter than its surface baffled astronomers for decades. After all, temperatures farther from a furnace are usually cooler than those closer. But recent accounts from a space-based solar observatory may have solved the mystery. Coronal loops vibrate wildly after being hit by the blast wave, or sun quake, of a solar flare. But, spacecraft observations showed, their vibration is quickly squelched, as if the loops were trying to vibrate in something thick like pudding rather than in a vacuum. That means the corona has a lot of friction. So when it damps (stops) the loops' vibration, the corona heats up—much as brakes heat up from friction in stopping a moving car or bicycle. In fact, this mechanism is amazingly efficient in transferring energy from the roiling surface of the Sun into the corona.

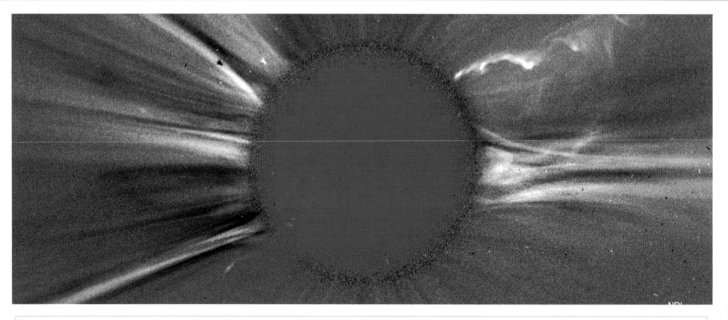

The Sun is gushing streams of gas particles at hundreds of miles per second out through the entire solar system—the solar wind. Some of the solar particles strike Earth's upper atmosphere, causing the auroras (northern or southern lights). Others spiral out into interplanetary and interstellar space.

Because the corona is so hot, its particles are whizzing around so fast that the Sun's enormous gravity can't even hold onto them. So the corona "breathes" charged particles into interplanetary space at incredible speeds—about 200 miles (300 km) per second over active regions and faster than 500 miles (800 km) per second over coronal holes near the poles. That's faster than 2 million miles (3 million km) an hour! These high-speed particles form the solar wind, which, as the Sun rotates, spirals out from the Sun through the entire solar system.

But that's not all. Roughly once a week during solar minimum and several times a day at solar maximum, the corona belches huge bubbles of gas threaded with magnetic fields, known as coronal mass ejections (CMEs). The CMEs disrupt the flow of the solar wind and produce disturbances that strike Earth and other planets. Although CMEs often accompany solar flares and eruptions of prominences, they can also occur without any obvious cause.

In other words, far more than the Sun's radiant energy bathes Earth. Our planet is buffeted by high- and low-speed streams of the solar wind, as well as is engulfed by bubbles of gas from CMEs.

This is the Sun's outer atmosphere as it appears in ultraviolet light emitted by ionized (electrically charged) oxygen atoms. The photo is a composite of two images made by two instruments aboard SOHO. Outside the black circle is the gas flowing away from the Sun to form the solar wind. Inside the black circle is the disk of the Sun itself, showing dark coronal holes at the poles and elsewhere, where the highest-speed solar wind originates.

With the Earth depending on the Sun for light, heat, and the sustenance of life, any minor variation in the Sun's energy output profoundly affects it. And as we've seen, the restless Sun varies continuously. So what happens when all these charged particles strike Earth?

The Sun's most well-known variation is its 11-year sunspot cycle, discovered by German astronomer Heinrich Schwabe around the time of the 1842 total solar eclipse. For two decades, Schwabe patiently turned his telescope to the Sun every clear day, diligently counting the sunspots he saw. In some years, whole days went by without any spots; in other years, there were dozens of spots every day, some so huge they were visible to the unaided eye. Even more importantly, Schwabe realized that the annual number of sunspots seemed to go from minimum to maximum and back to minimum in about 11 years.

By the late 19th century, astronomers strongly suspected that the sunspot cycle had a profound effect on Earth. In the years the Sun's face was peppered with sunspots, the nighttime skies over northern North America and Europe danced with ghostly green and red auroras (northern lights), fluttering like enormous draperies in a breeze. Sometimes auroras, normally seen only at high latitudes, were spotted as far south as California or Florida. During the most dramatic displays, communications were disrupted

he Sun's magnetic fields and releases of plasma can engulf Earth, which is protected rimarily by its own magnetic field (blue lines). In this illustration, a magnetic cloud of asma from the Sun is approaching Earth. White lines represent the solar wind and the urple line is the bow shock (where the supersonic solar wind meets Earth's magnetic field). he sizes of the Sun and Earth and the distance between them are not shown to scale.

31

on the telegraph wires that crisscrossed the United States and Europe, and sparks would discharge from the telegraph keys. Even today, auroras at sunspot maximum interfere with radio and television reception and temporarily knock out satellite communications.

What's happening?

At sunspot maximum, when the Sun is ceaselessly erupting with flares, prominences, and coronal mass ejections, record concentrations of charged particles are spewed into the solar wind. Those particles arrive at Earth a few days later, becoming trapped in Earth's magnetic field and spiraling along magnetic

Curtains of the aurora borealis, or northern lights, taking the momentary shape of a ring that seems to be hovering just above the trees on October 6, 2002, are actually 60 miles (100 km) or more above Earth. The greenish glow is produced when energetic electrons from the Sun (the solar wind) plow into oxygen molecules in Earth's upper atmosphere, causing the air molecules to fluoresce (emit light).

field lines toward the north and south poles. When the solar particles collide with air molecules high in Earth's tenuous upper atmosphere (50 miles (80 km) high and higher), they ionize (strip electrons from) the air molecules. When the ionized molecules recombine with their freed electrons, they emit photons (particles of light). In short, the air molecules glow, becoming visible as the flickering auroras.

The Sun actually glows slightly (about 0.1 percent) brighter at sunspot maximum than at sunspot minimum. That's not much, but it's enough to affect Earth. For example, shortly after Galileo first turned his telescope sunward, sunspots virtually disappeared! Almost none were seen between 1645 and 1715, even though the Sun was observed regularly by capable astronomers with decent telescopes. On Earth, gone also were flickering auroras. More dramatically, those 70 years of solar inactivity—and thus a slightly cooler Sun—corresponded to the "Little Ice Age," a cold climatic period during which rivers in Europe and the United States that didn't normally ice up froze solid, and snow fields remained year-round at low altitudes.

What causes the sunspot cycle? Why does it last about 11 years? And what makes it sometimes "turn off"? Those are great solar mysteries yet to be solved!

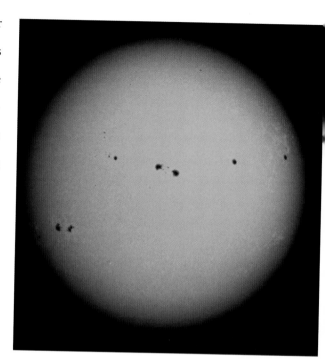

Sunspots are often seen on the Sun's photosphere (visible face). Here, two large sunspots appear together in the center. Because sunspots are about half as bright as the surrounding photosphere, they seem dark by contrast. Bright faculae, which appear in regions just before sunspots form, are visible near the Sun's limb (edge).

Peabody Public Library
Columbia City, IN

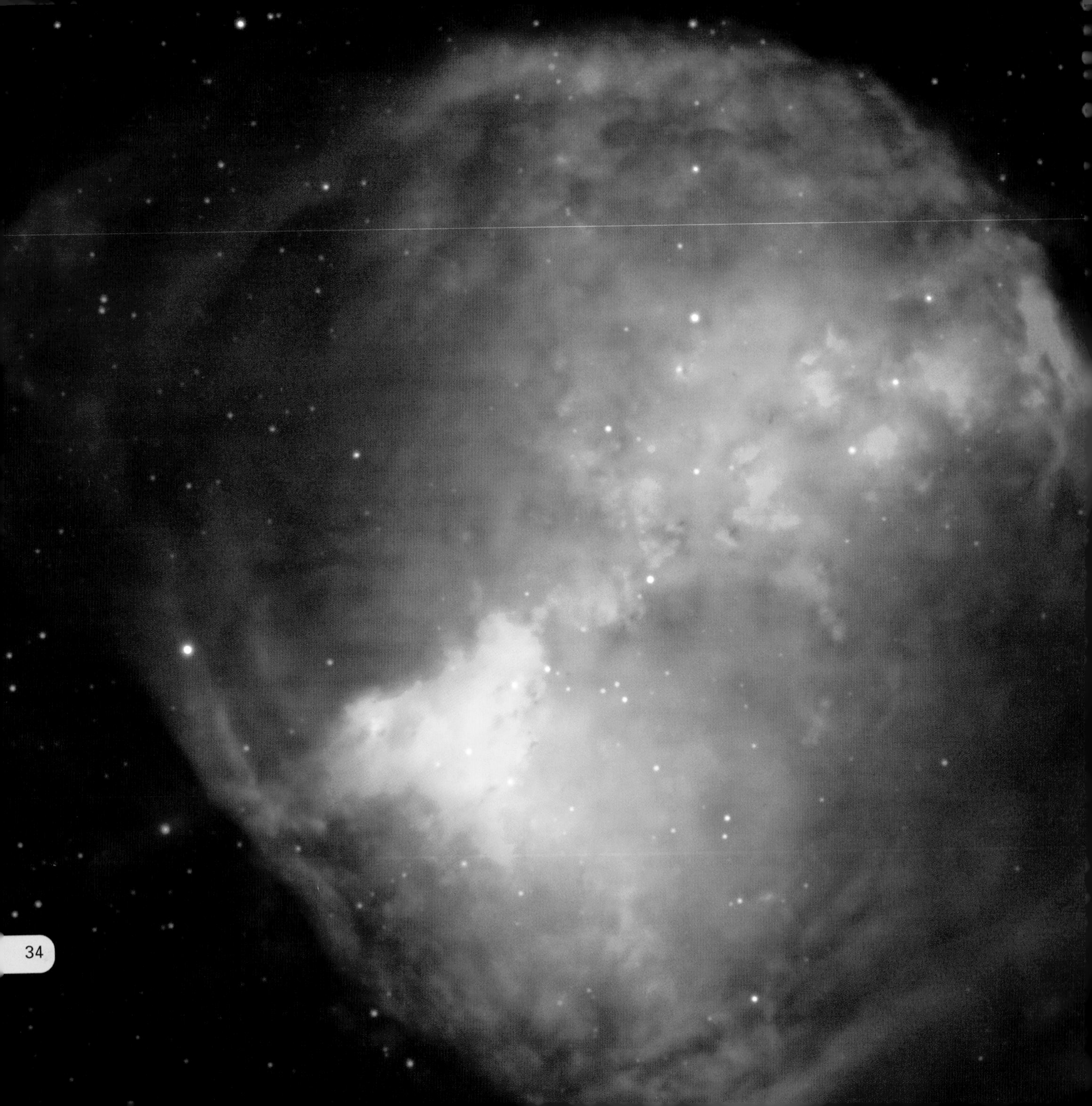

The Sun as a "Middle-Aged" Star

As important as the Sun is to life on Earth and as turbulent as it appears from close up, compared with the rest of the universe, it's actually a very stable, well-behaved, ordinary star.

Yes, the Sun is a star, kin to all the other stars you see glowing in the night sky. If you compared all the stars in our galaxy at the same distance, you'd see that the Sun is neither the brightest nor the dimmest, neither the largest nor the smallest, neither the youngest nor the oldest. That's very lucky for us, of course. Had the Sun been big and bright and hot, it would have burned through its nuclear fuel in only a few hundred million years—not enough time for Earth to have cooled, and plants, animals, and humans to have evolved. Had it been small and dim and cool, Earth might have been just too dark and frigid for life as we know it.

Evidence and best estimates put the Sun's age at about 4.5 billion years, less than halfway through its estimated lifetime. In other words, the Sun is a healthy, middle-aged star in its prime.

So how much longer will the sun live?

Astronomers give it at least another 5 billion years of fusing hydrogen into helium, much as it's doing now (although, over time, doubling in brightness).

Dumbbell Nebula, a planetary nebula in the constellation Vulpecula, formed when a red giant star near the end of its life ejected its outer gaseous envelope. The expanding, spherical cloud of gas is visible because ultraviolet light from the star's hot core (a white dwarf), visible near the center, ionizes the cloud and causes it to glow. At the end of the Sun's life, it, too, will swell up into a red giant and puff off its outer layers.

The Sun's "Rainbow"

A high-resolution spectrum of the Sun that shows the complete range of colors visible to the unaided eye (wavelengths from 400 to 700 nanometers) is produced by passing sunlight through a prismlike device. The spectrum is made up of a sequence of 50 horizontal strips, each strip covering 6 nanometers. It shows that although the Sun emits light of nearly every color, it is brightest in yellow-green light. Short, vertical black lines crossing each strip are Fraunhofer lines—"missing" wavelengths in which gases at or above the photosphere absorb light; from these spectral lines, it is possible to determine the gases that compose the Sun.

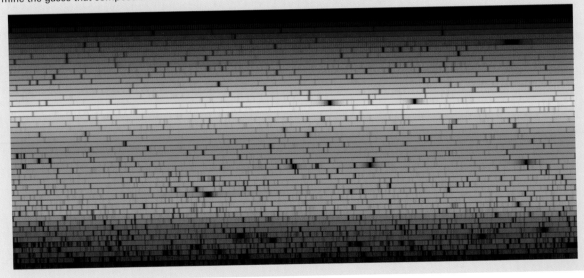

When its core runs out of hydrogen, the Sun will burn its helium ashes into heavier elements. This process will cause it to swell into a red giant star so huge that it will engulf the orbits of the solar system's first three planets, destroying any life still on Earth. After another billion years or so, it will puff off its outer layers as a planetary nebula (a spherical cloud of gas that looks like a planet), and its inner layers will collapse into a white dwarf—the end of a star of the Sun's mass. The white dwarf will then slowly cool to yellow, orange, red, and then brown before darkening altogether into a cold stellar cinder, fading away like the embers of a campfire.

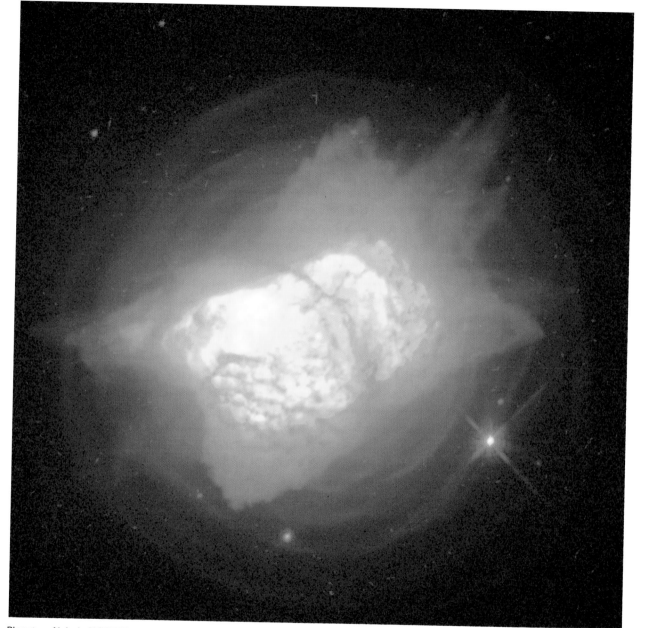

Planetary Nebula NGC 7027 as seen by the *Hubble Space Telescope* reveals new features of the spectacular death throes of a star about the mass of the Sun. New features include: several faint, blue, concentric shells surrounding the nebula (indicating the star initially ejected gas several times); an extensive network of red dust clouds throughout the bright inner region (indicating one last vigorous ejection); and the hot central white dwarf, visible as a white dot at the center.

"Chasing" Solar Eclipses and Other Projects

Want to observe the Sun and count some sunspots yourself? You can, as long as you heed one cardinal rule: *Never look directly at the Sun!* Without adequate protection, the Sun can blind you by damaging your retinas.

The safest way to observe the Sun is indirectly: by projecting its image onto a screen. Then you can study the image on the screen for as long as you like.

A pinhole projector is the easiest and cheapest method, and it uses materials you likely have right in your own home: a few shoeboxes with lids, black paint, a bit of aluminum foil, tape, a needle and a piece of white paper. Paint the insides of all the shoeboxes and their lids flat black. After they dry, cut 2-inch (5 cm) holes into all the ends of the shoeboxes except for one. Tape all the shoeboxes into a long, square tube with the single uncut end at the bottom. Cover the top hole with a small square of aluminum foil. Carefully insert a needle into the foil, leaving a tiny round hole (this is your pinhole). Inside the uncut end of the shoebox opposite the pinhole, tape a square of white paper (this is your projection screen). Tape all the lids onto the shoebox tube. In the side of the tube near the projection screen, cut a small hole for your eye. Now, point the pinhole toward the Sun and look through the eyehole at the projection screen to see a projected image of it.

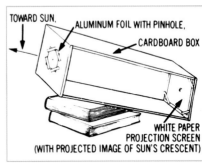

The drawing above shows a version of a pinhole projector using a single shoebox with the lid off.

On June 30, 1973, some 200 members of Amateur Astronomers Inc., from Cranford, New Jersey, set up telescopes in the courtyard and on the roof of a school in Akjoujt, Mauritania, in the middle of the Sahara, to photograph the longest total eclipse of the Sun in the 20th century—more than seven minutes.

The shoebox pinhole projector is good enough to see large sunspots and track their progress from day to day across the Sun's face. It's also handy for watching the partial phases of a solar eclipse and for watching rare transits of Mercury and Venus, when those planets come directly between Earth and the Sun. *But remember: Do not look directly through the pinhole at the Sun.*

For viewing sunspots in more detail, as well as seeing finer features (granules, supergranules, faculae, etc.) on the surface of the Sun, you'll need some actual optics instead of a pinhole. Again, the simplest method is projection, using half of a pair of binoculars and a white card as a projection screen. The lenses can be focused to give a larger and sharper solar image than is possible with a pinhole. An even larger image can be projected using a cheap department-store telescope. Improve the image's contrast by surrounding the white projection screen with a box sealed with tape and painted black to absorb stray light. *Do NOT look directly through the binoculars or telescope at the Sun.*

To experience the excitement of viewing the Sun's ruby prominences and the ghostly corona of a total eclipse in the United States or Canada, you'll have to wait until August 21, 2017. But if you (and your family) are willing to travel to other parts of the world, you'll have 11 opportunities between now and then. Several organizations—among them the National Geographic Society in Washington, D.C.; *Sky & Telescope* magazine in Cambridge, Massachusetts; some major science museums; planetariums; astronomy clubs; and specialized tour agencies—take paying guests on eclipse expeditions that range from camping trips to luxury cruises.

This image of the total solar eclipse on February 6, 1980, was photographed in Hyderabad, India. The Moon's black disk is ringed by the Sun's corona.

Although solar eclipses are very rare on Earth, from space the crew of *Apollo 12* was able to catch this dramatic view of the Sun peeking around Earth's limb as they traveled home from the moon in November of 1969.

Total Solar Eclipses 2003–2017

The Sun is eclipsed by the Moon at least twice every year, with the partial phases visible from an area thousands of miles wide and long across Earth. Only some solar eclipses are total, where the Moon completely covers the Sun's blinding disk. Those that are can be seen only from within a narrow path swept from west to east across Earth by the tip of the darkest central cone of the Moon's shadow (the umbra). Although also thousands of miles long, this path of totality is always less than 170 miles (274 km) wide and is usually much narrower: visualize a string draped in an arc over a terrestrial globe. From any spot on Earth, totality never lasts longer than seven and one-half minutes and is usually much shorter.

The last total solar eclipse across the continental United States occurred in 1979; the next one will occur in 2017. Below is a table of all the total solar eclipses between 2003 and 2017. *Central Duration* means "the length of totality at greatest eclipse in minutes and seconds." *Hybrid* means "the eclipse will be both total and annular (leaving a bright ring or annulus around the moon) along its central path." *Geographic Region of Eclipse Visibility* is the portion of Earth on which the eclipse can be seen.

Date	Eclipse Type	Central Duration	Geographic Region of Eclipse Visability
2003, November 23	Total	1m 57s	Australia, New Zealand, Antarctica, S. America
2005, April 8	Hybrid	0m 42s	New Zealand, N. and S. America; South Pacific, Panama, Colombia, Venezuela
2006, March 29	Total	4m 07s	Africa, Europe, W. Asia; central Africa, Turkey, Russia
2008, August 1	Total	2m 27s	N. America, Europe, Asia; northern Canada, Greenland, Siberia, Mongolia, China
2009, July 22	Total	6m 39s	E. Asia, Pacific Ocean, Hawaii; India, Nepal, China, central Pacific
2010, July 11	Total	5m 20s	southern S. America; South Pacific, Easter Island, Chile, Argentina
2012, November 13	Total	4m 02s	Australia, New Zealand, South Pacific, southern S. America; northern Australia
2013, November 3	Hybrid	1m 40s	central Americas, southern Europe, Africa, Atlantic, central Africa
2015, March 20	Total	2m 47s	Iceland, Europe, northern Africa, northern Asia; northern Atlantic, Faeroe Island, Svalbard
2016, March 9	Total	4m 09s	Central Asia, Australia, Pacific; Sumatra, Borneo, Sulawesi
2017, August 21	Total	2m 40s	N. America, northern S. America; northern Pacific, southern Atlantic

Further Information

Bell, Trudy E., "The Victorian Space Program,"
    The Bent, vol. 94, no. 2, pp. 11–18 (Spring
    2003).

Garlick, Mark A., "Starspots," *Sky & Telescope*,
    vol. 101, no. 3, pp. 42–46 (March 2001).

Littmann, Mark, Ken Willcox, and Fred Espenak,
    Totality: *Eclipses of the Sun*, (Oxford
    University Press, second edition, 1999)
.
Odenwald, Sten, "Solar Storms: The Silent
    Menace," *Sky & Telescope*, vol. 99, no. 3,
    pp. 50–56 (March 2000).

Pasachoff, Jay M., "Solar-Eclipse Science: Still
    Going Strong," *Sky & Telescope*, vol. 101,
    no. 2, pp. 40–47 (February 2001).

Schrijver, Carolus J. and Alan M. Title, "Today's
    Science of the Sun," part I in S*ky &
    Telescope*, vol. 101, no. 2, pp. 34–39
    (February 2001); part II in S*ky &
    Telescope*, vol. 101, no. 3, pp. 34–40
    (March 2001).

Zirker, Jack B., *Journey from the Center of the Sun*,
    (Princeton University Press, 2001).

Home page for "The Nine Planets: A
    Multimedia Tour of the Solar System"
    http://seds.lpl.arizona.edu/nineplanets/
    nineplanets/nineplanets.html

NASA Goddard Spaceflight Center Eclipse home
    page
    http://sunearth.gsfc.nasa.gov/eclipse/
    eclipse.html

Science@NASA news home page (for all branches
    of astronomy and space science)
    http://science.nasa.gov

NASA Marshall Space Flight Center Solar
    Physics site
    http://science.nasa.gov/ssl/pad/solar

Solar and Heliospheric Observatory (SOHO)
    home page
    http://sohowww.nascom.nasa.gov

Views of the Solar System photo archive for the
    Sun
    http://www.solarviews.com/cap/index/
    sun1.html

Glossary

aurora—The red and green aurora borealis, or northern lights, frequently seen at high northern latitudes (and at high southern latitudes, as the aurora australis, or "southern lights") when charged particles from the Sun interact with Earth's magnetic field and atmosphere.

chromosphere—The thin, irregular, red layer of the Sun's outer atmosphere just above the photosphere, in which prominences originate.

chromospheric network—The network of bright and dark features in the chromosphere over the Sun's face that frequently outline supergranules.

convection cells—Areas of the Sun that are "boiling" to convey heat and energy from deeper layers.

convective zone, solar—The region between the Sun's radiative zone and the photosphere, which is opaque to photons (particles of light and other electromagnetic radiation); energy travels through this zone toward the Sun's surface principally by convection, or the "boiling" movement of masses of hot material.

core, solar—The "engine room" of the Sun, where hydrogen nuclei fuse into helium nuclei, liberating prodigious amounts of energy.

corona—The outermost atmosphere of the Sun, visible from Earth during total solar eclipses as a beautiful, pearly halo with spikes and streamers; parts of the corona are as hot as the Sun's interior.

Coronal mass ejections (CMEs)—Huge bubbles of ionized gas "belched" into space from the corona.

density—Density equals the mass (weight) of a material divided by its volume. It is the measure of the relative pull on an object by gravity.

differential rotation—The nonsolid pattern of the Sun's rotation, in which the equatorial regions complete one rotation days ahead of higher latitudes.

eclipse—An astronomical event when one object either totally or partially blocks another object from view.

faculae—Bright spots on the Sun near sunspots; they often form over areas where sunspots will appear.

fusion—A thermonuclear reaction that liberates tremendous energy, usually when two hydrogen nuclei are combined under pressure to form one helium nucleus.

granules—California- or Texas-sized convection cells in the Sun's photosphere.

gravity—One of the four basic forces of nature, the force that attracts masses to each other.

H-alpha emission—Red light emitted by a certain transition of hydrogen and characteristic of the chromosphere.

ionization—The stripping of electrons from neutral atoms to create charged particles (ions), both negatively charged electrons and positively charged atomic nuclei.

limb—The apparent edge of the Sun (or other celestial body) projected onto the sky.

limb darkening—The tendency of the limb of the Sun to look dark because an observer on Earth is seeing obliquely through layers of gas, which absorb some light.

magnetic field—An area of magnetic influence that circulates between the two poles of a magnet.

mass—The weight of an object that changes as the force of gravity changes.

nuclear fusion—Splitting the nucleus of an atom so that it releases energy.

photosphere—The Sun's visible surface as seen from Earth.

plages—Bright patches in the chromospheric network surrounding sunspots.

proton—A subatomic particle in the nucleus of an atom. Protons have a positive charge.

radiation—Energy that travels via electromagnetic waves. Some radiation is dangerous, some is not. Radiation from the Sun provides heat and light. Radiation from x-rays can damage tissue.

radiative zone, solar—The region between the Sun's core and its convective zone, where energy travels toward the surface principally by radiation.

solar maximum—Years during the sunspot cycle when the Sun's face has many sunspots, indicating great magnetic activity.

solar minimum—Years during the sunspot cycle when the Sun's face has few or no sunspots and there is little magnetic activity.

solar wind—A continuous stream of charged particles that are released from the Sun and hurled outward into space at speeds up to 500 miles (800 km) per second.

spicules—Small, spiky, jetlike eruptions in the chromosphere lasting only a few minutes.

sunspot—A colossal magnetic storm in the photosphere that is cooler than the surrounding surface and so looks dark from Earth; the largest sunspots can be many times larger than Earth.

sunspot cycle—A cycle in the annual number of sunspots, going from minimum to maximum and back to minimum in an average period of 11 years.

supergranules—Huge convection zones in the photosphere as large as sunspots.

tachocline—The thin region inside the Sun that separates the radiative zone from the convective zone and is believed to be the source of the Sun's magnetic field.

Index

Peabody Public Library
Columbia City, IN

Peabody Public Library
Columbia City, IN